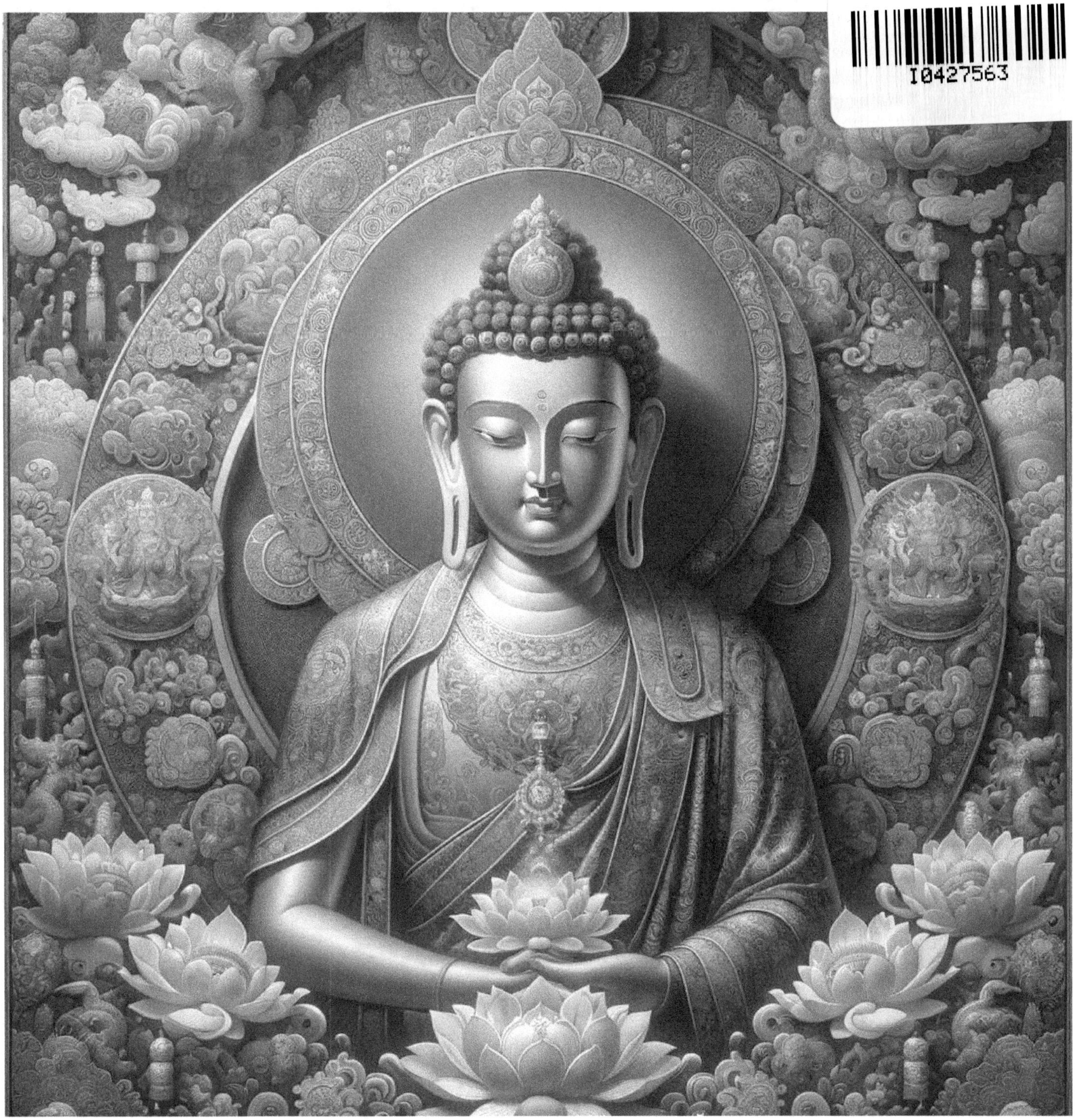

# Buddhist Figures

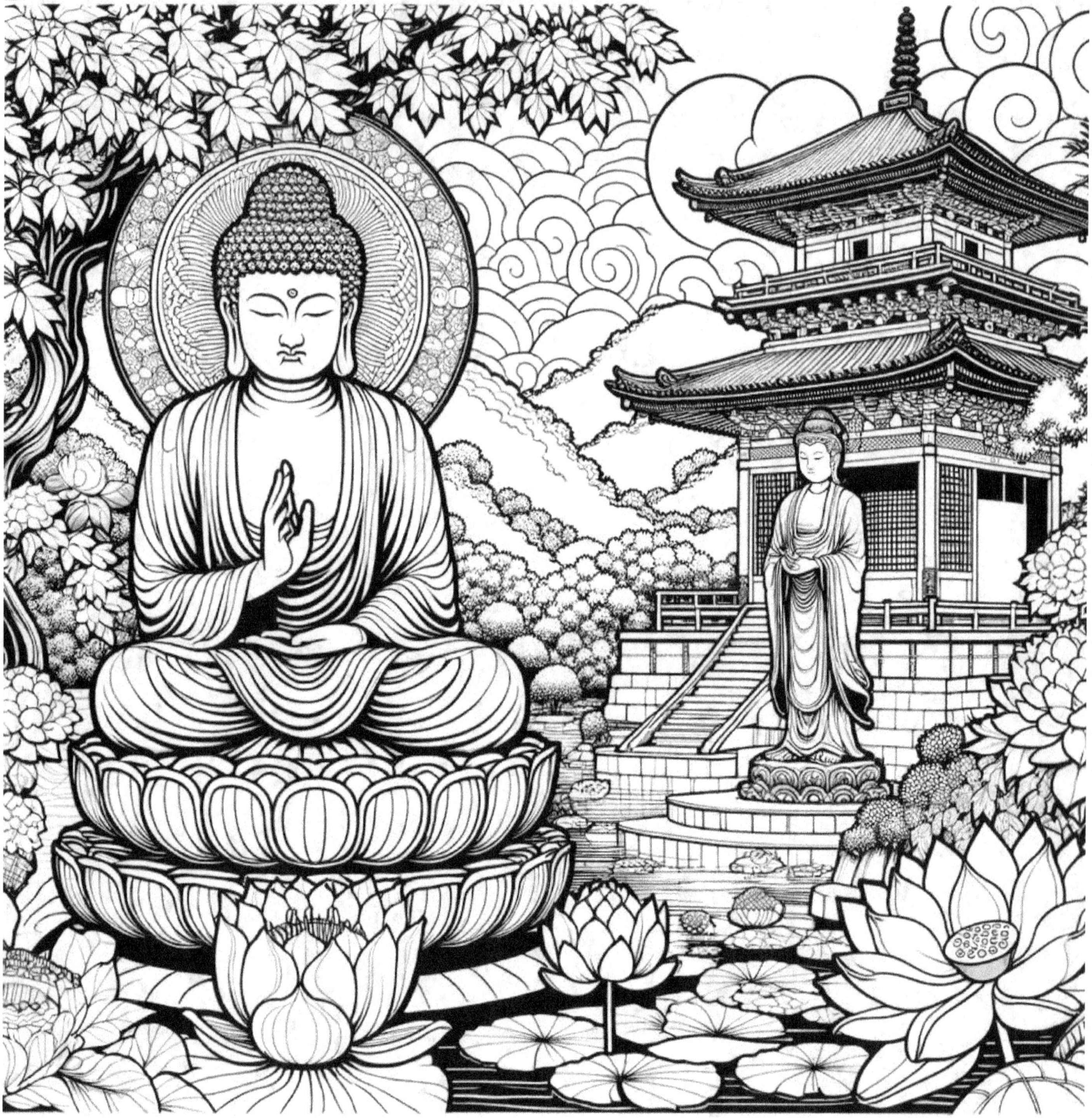

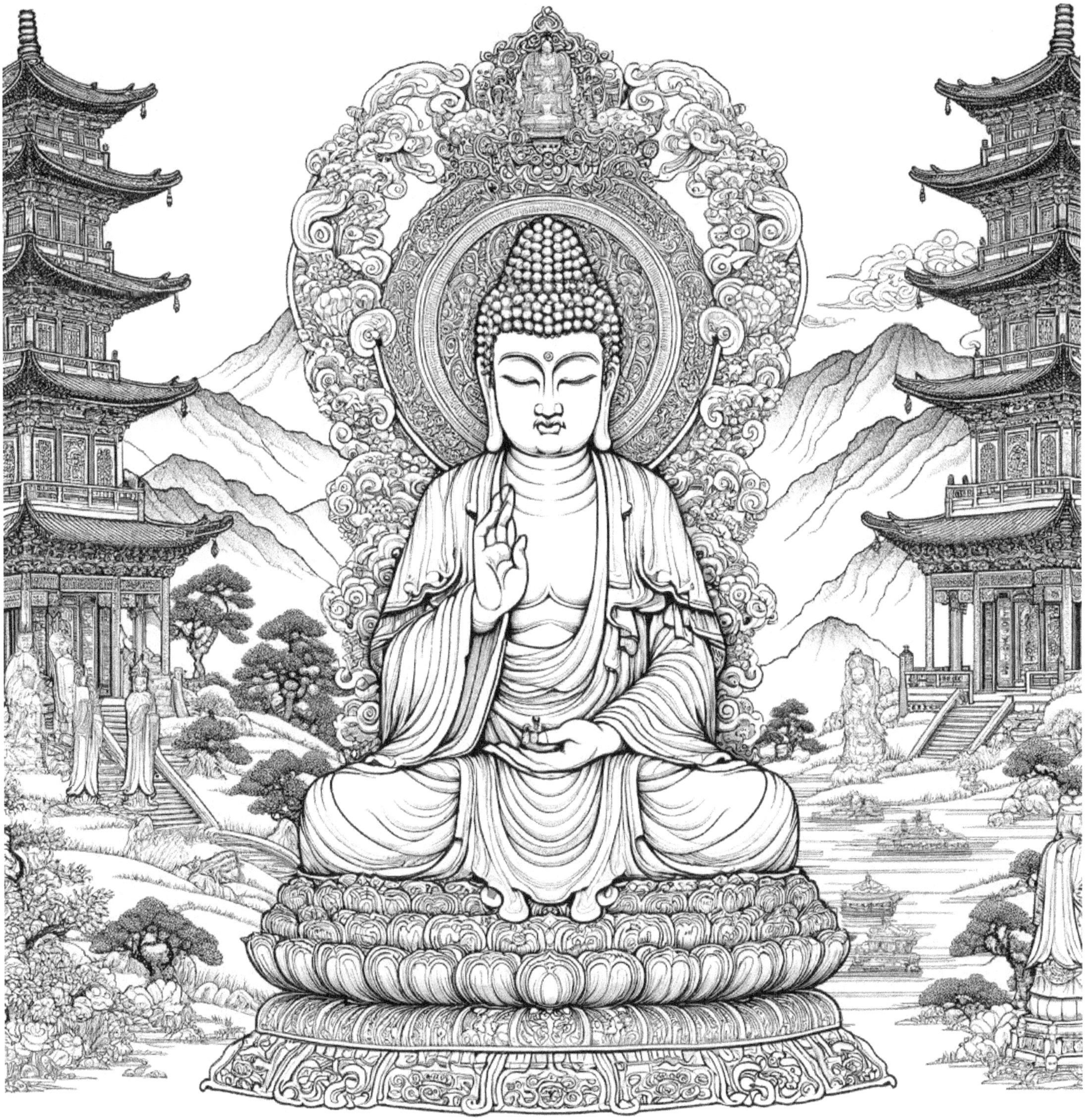

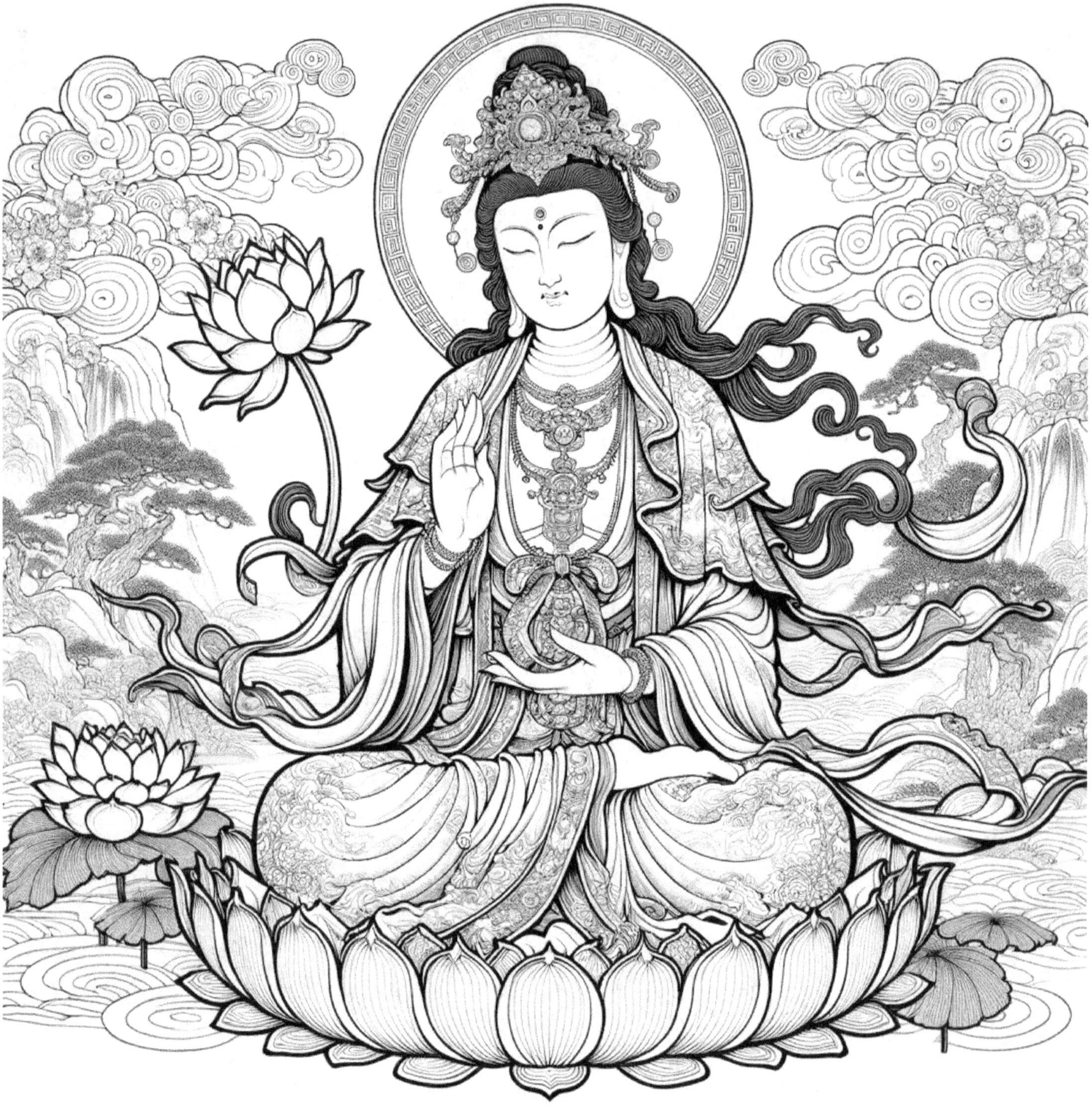

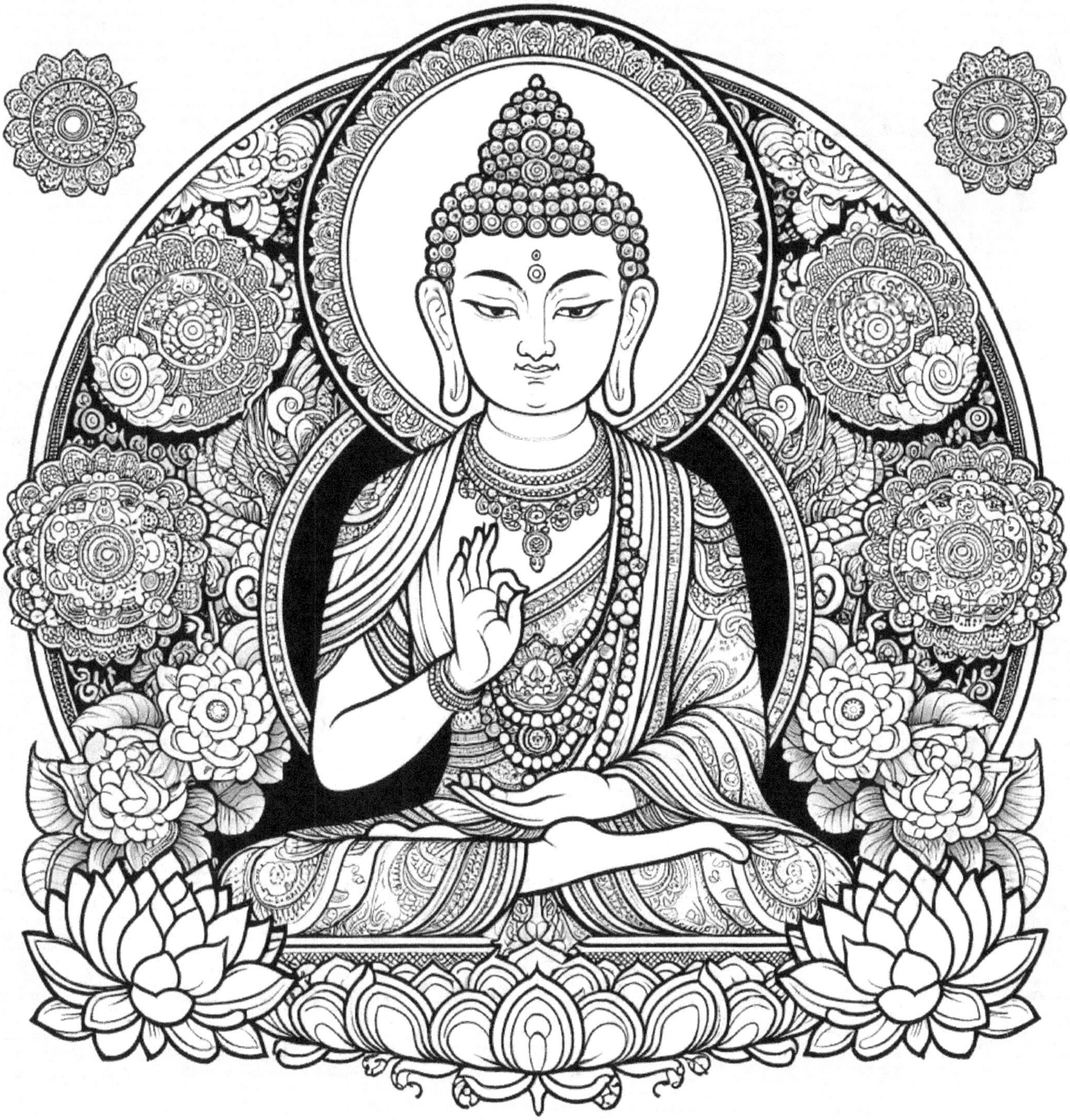

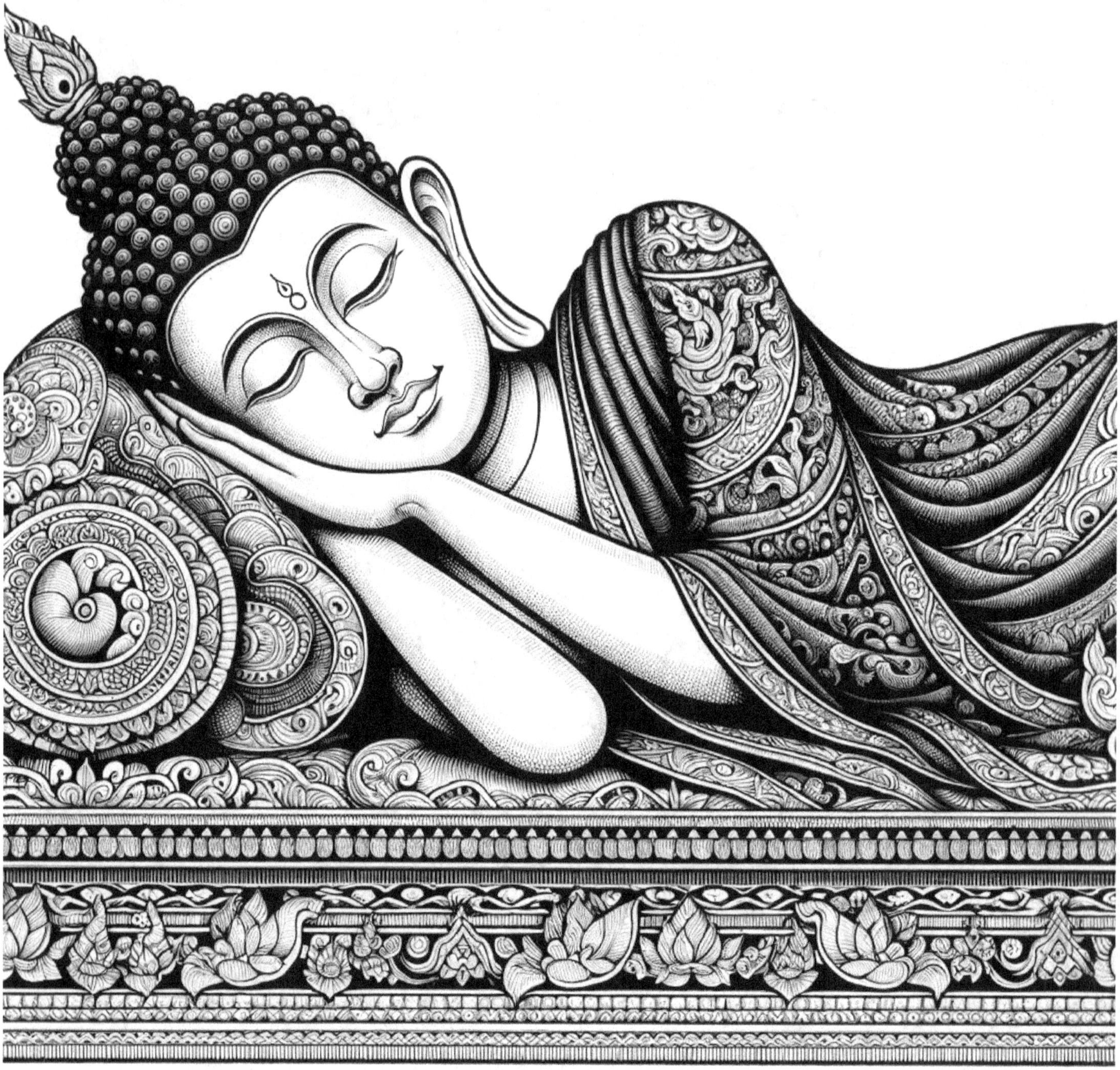

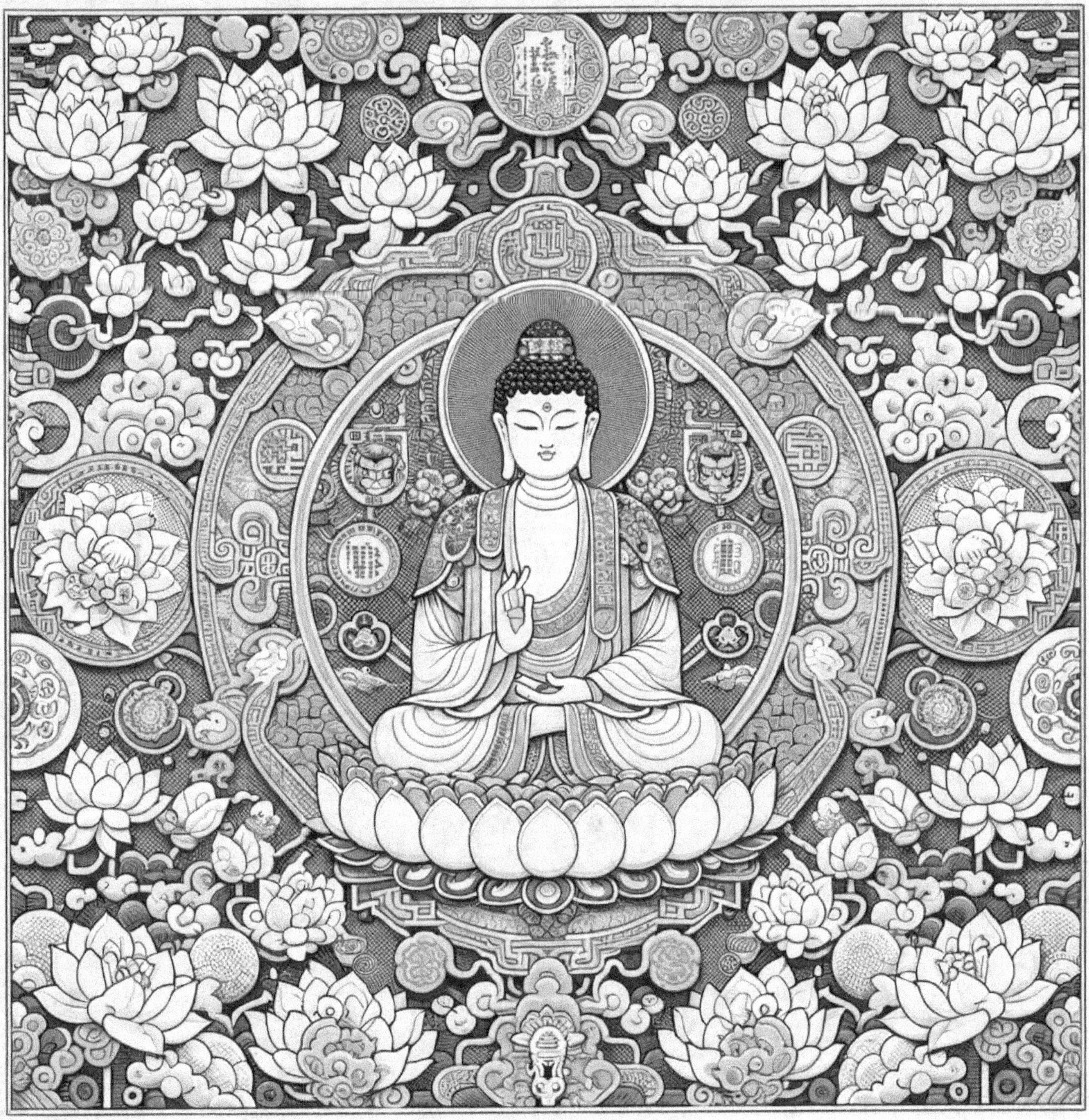

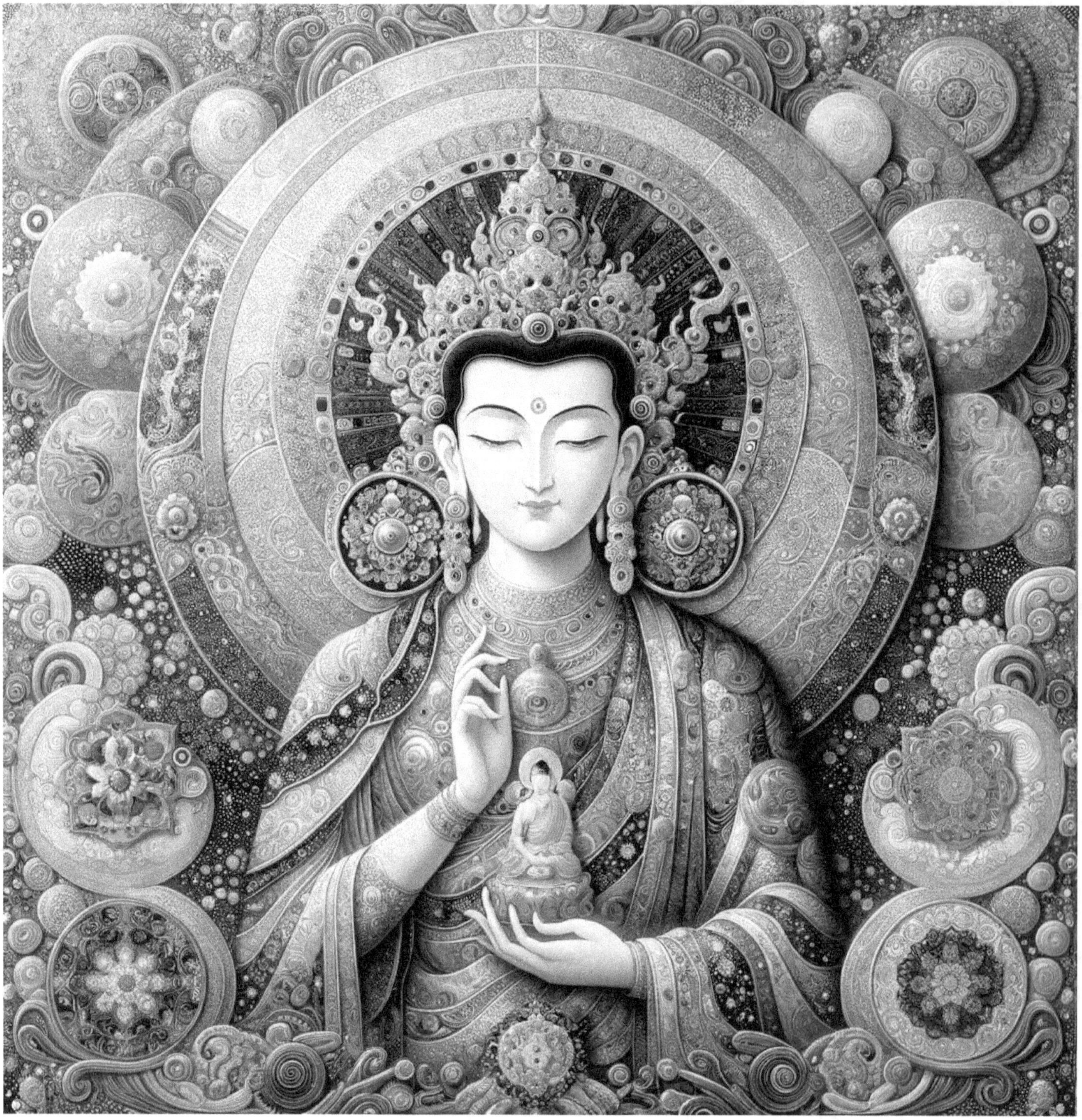

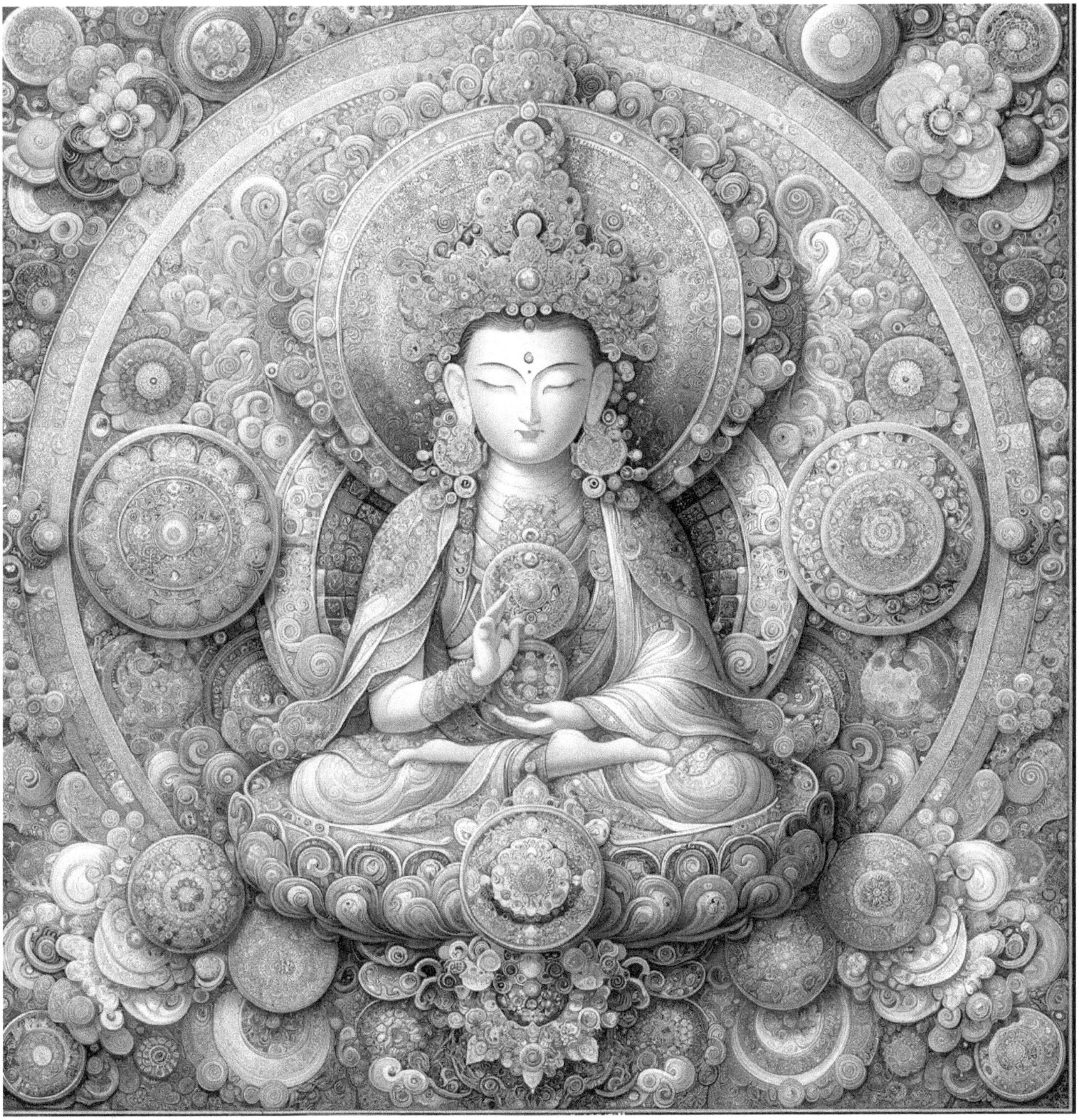

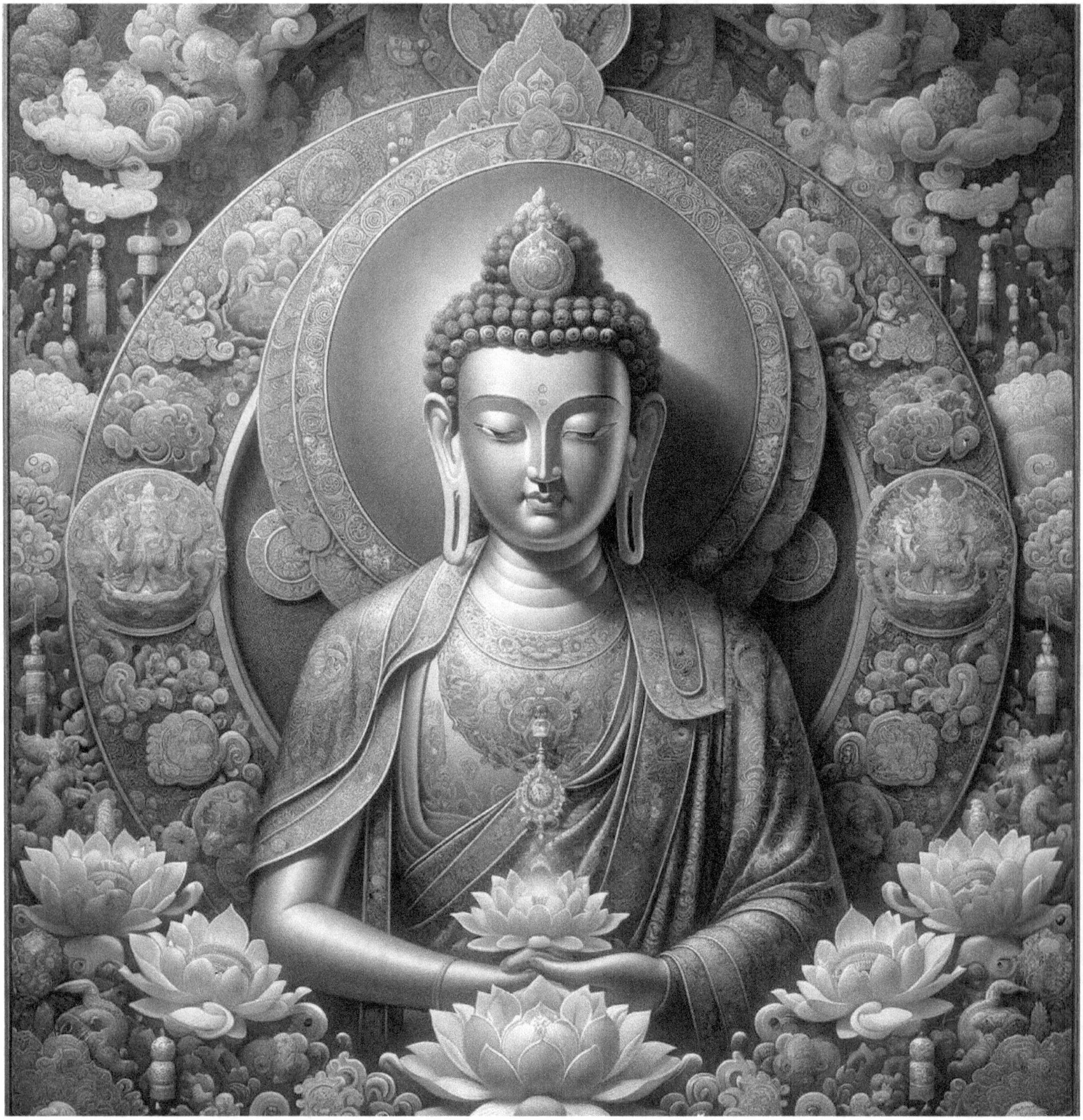

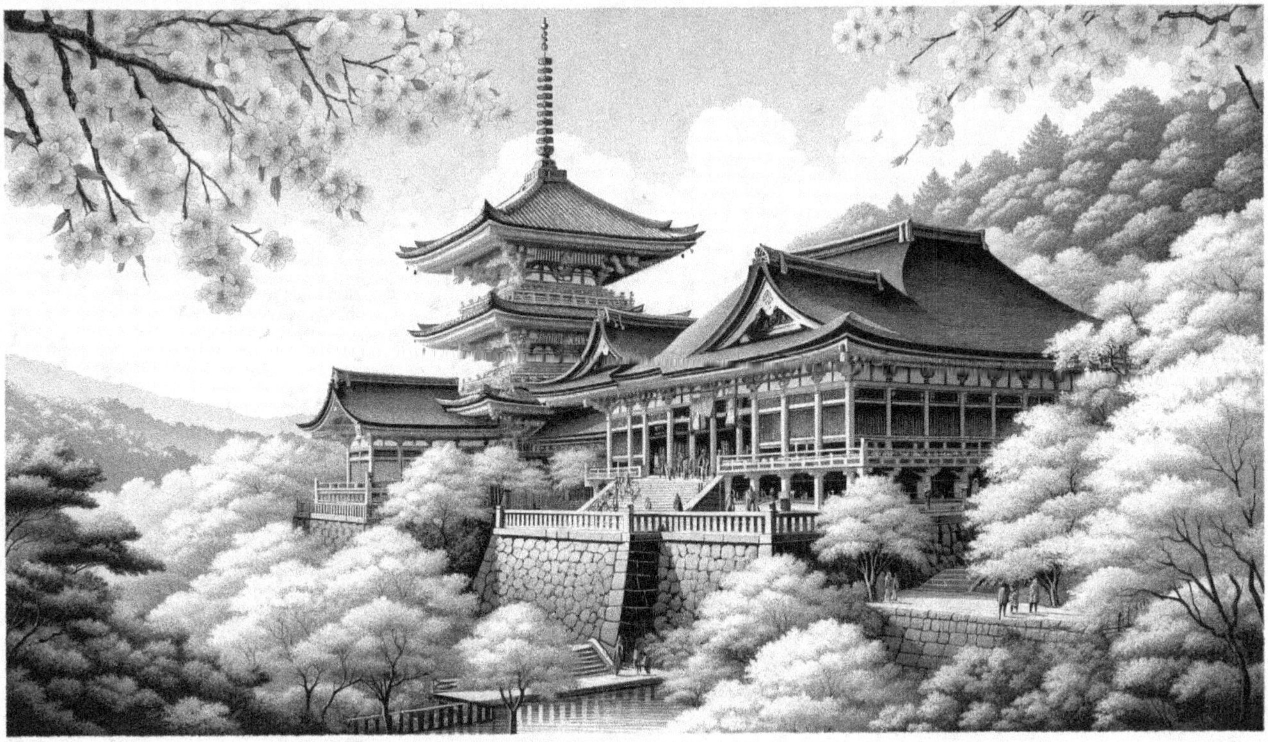

# East Asian Temples

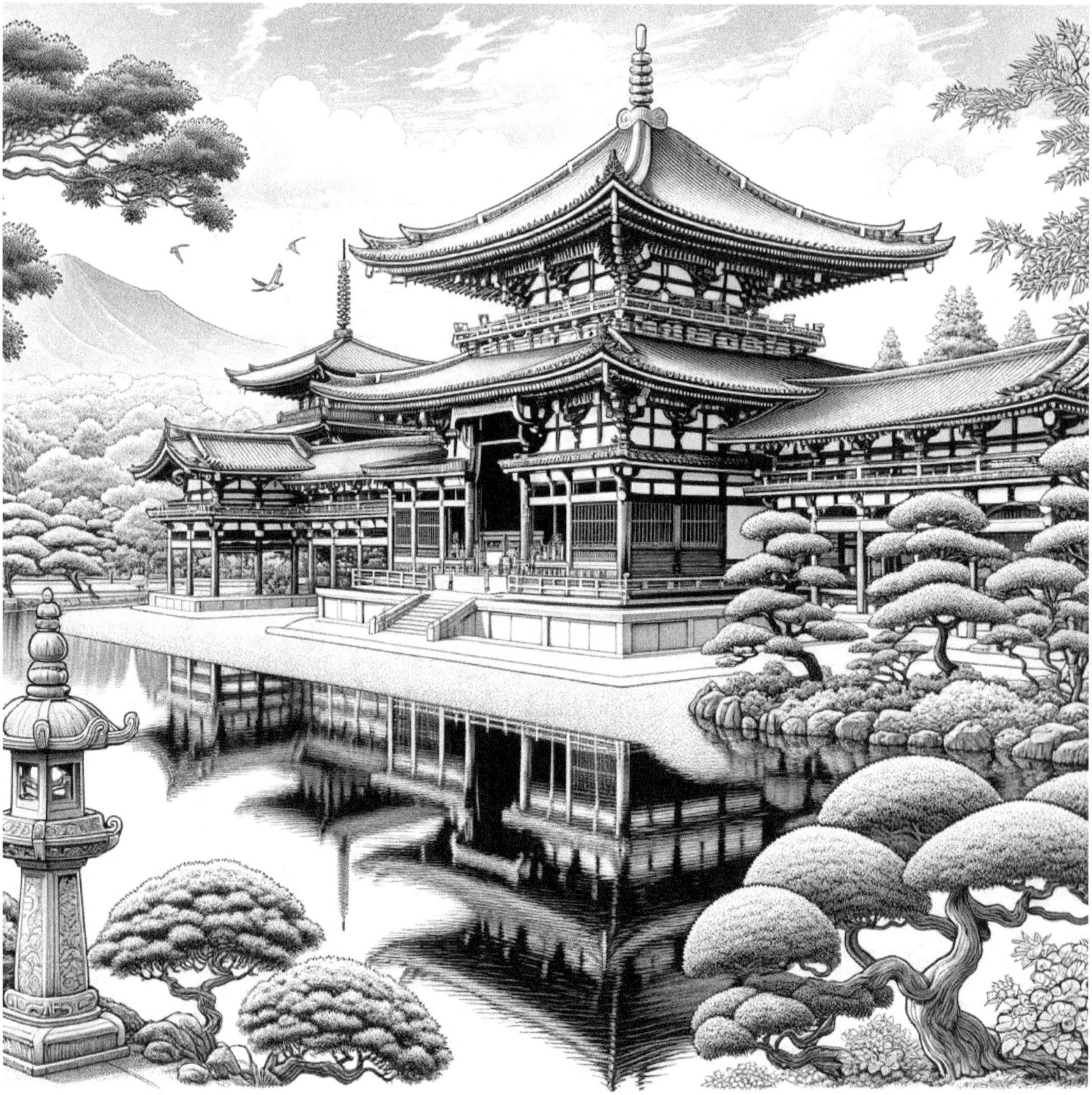

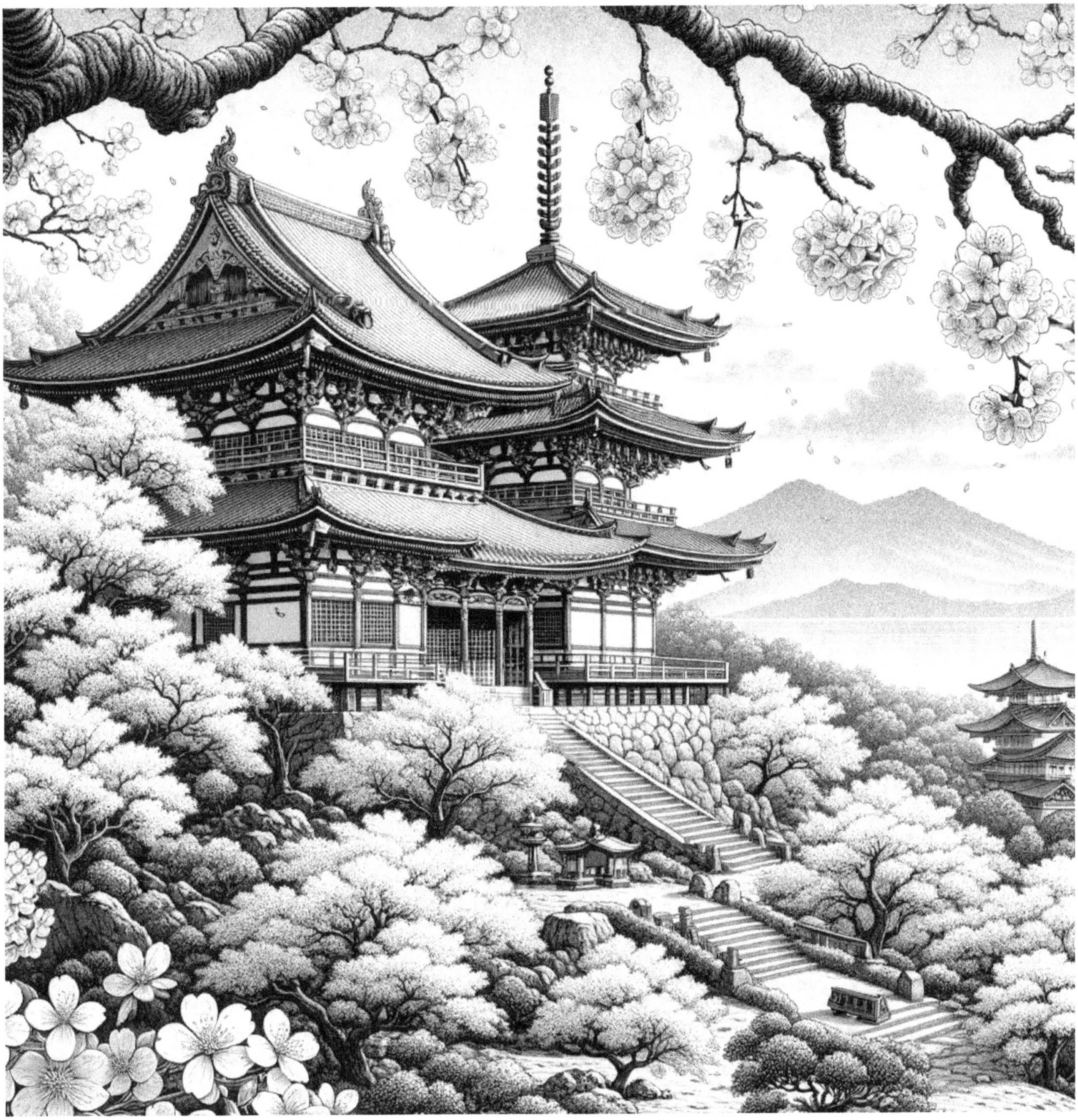

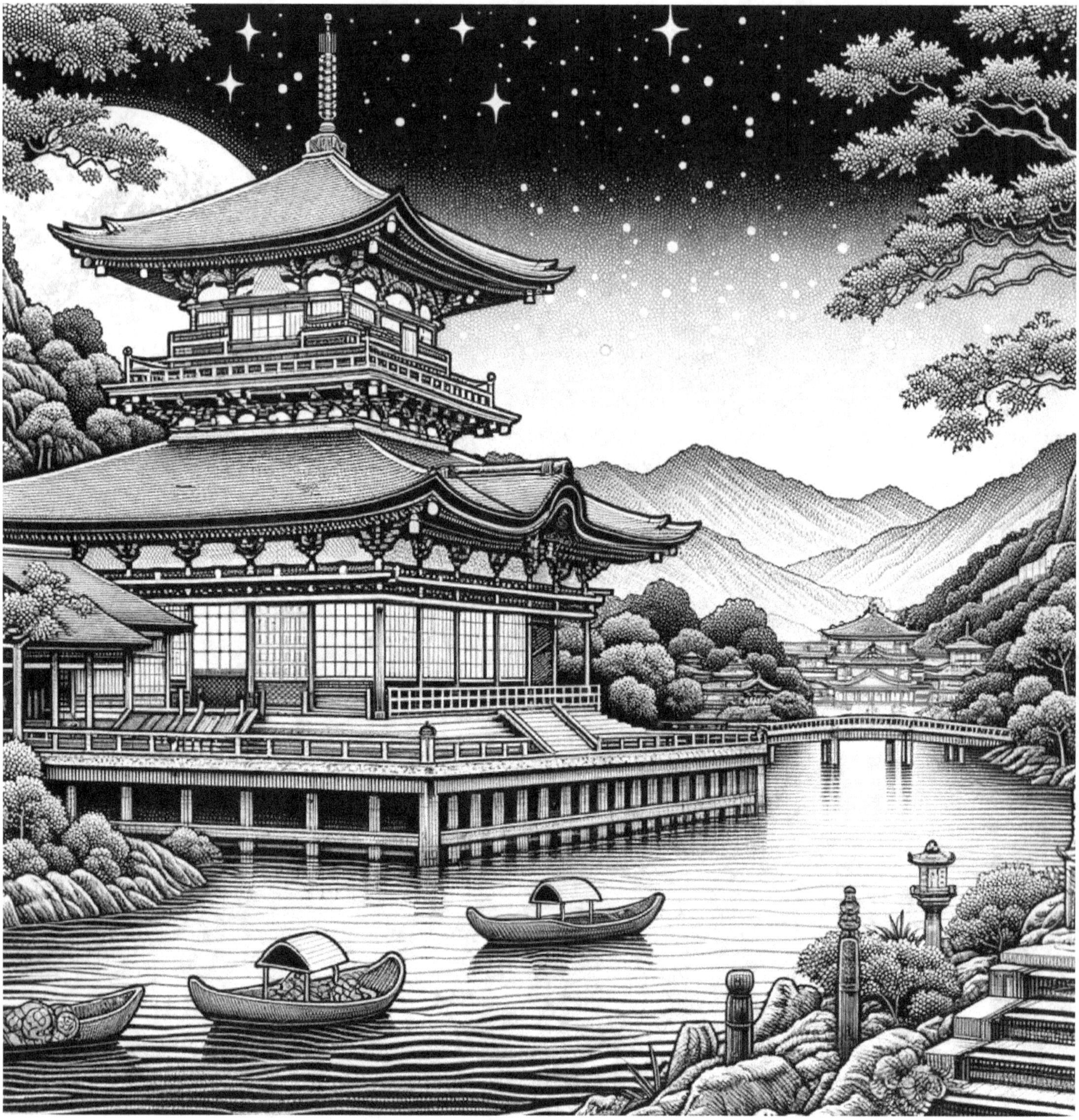

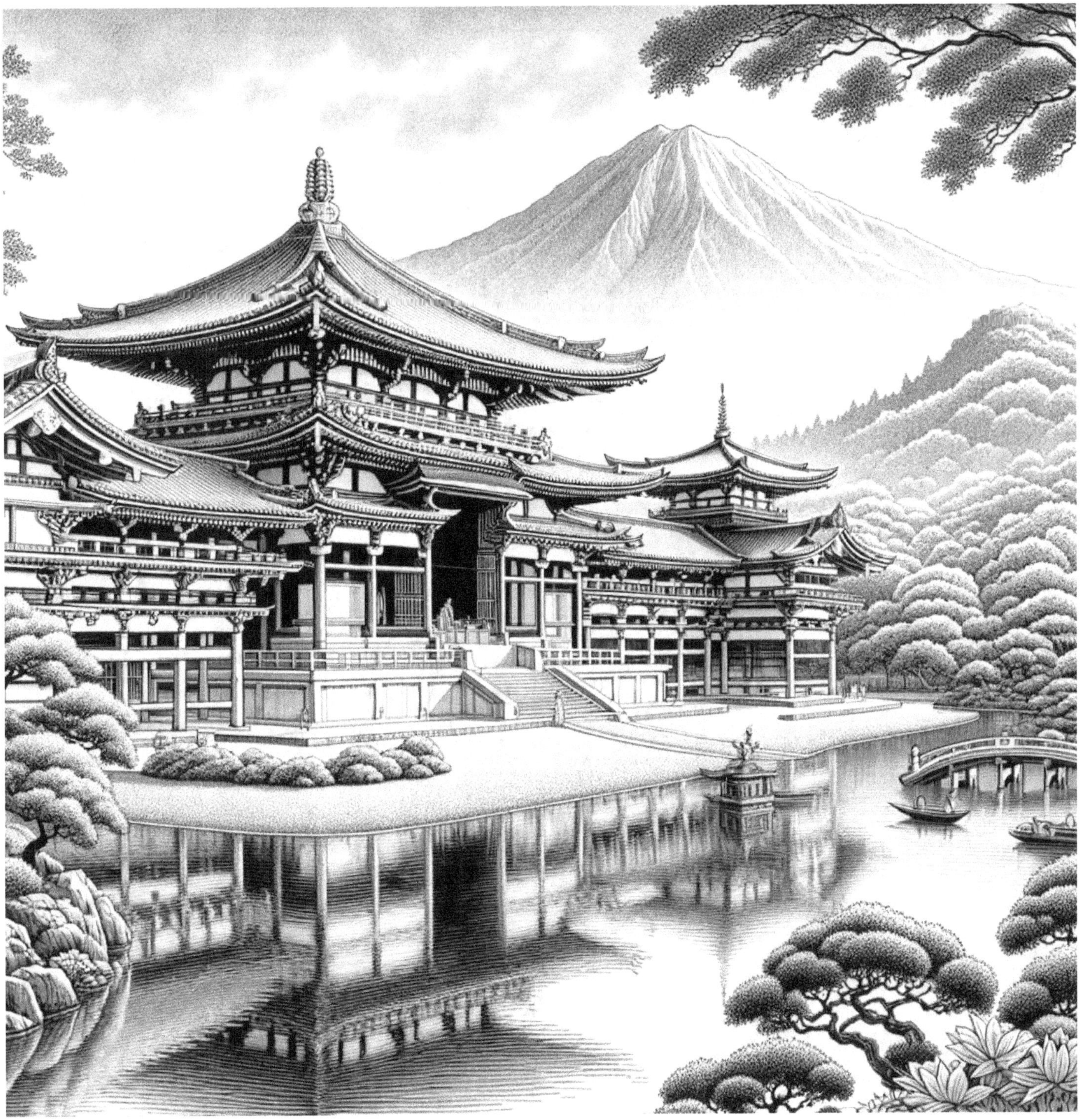

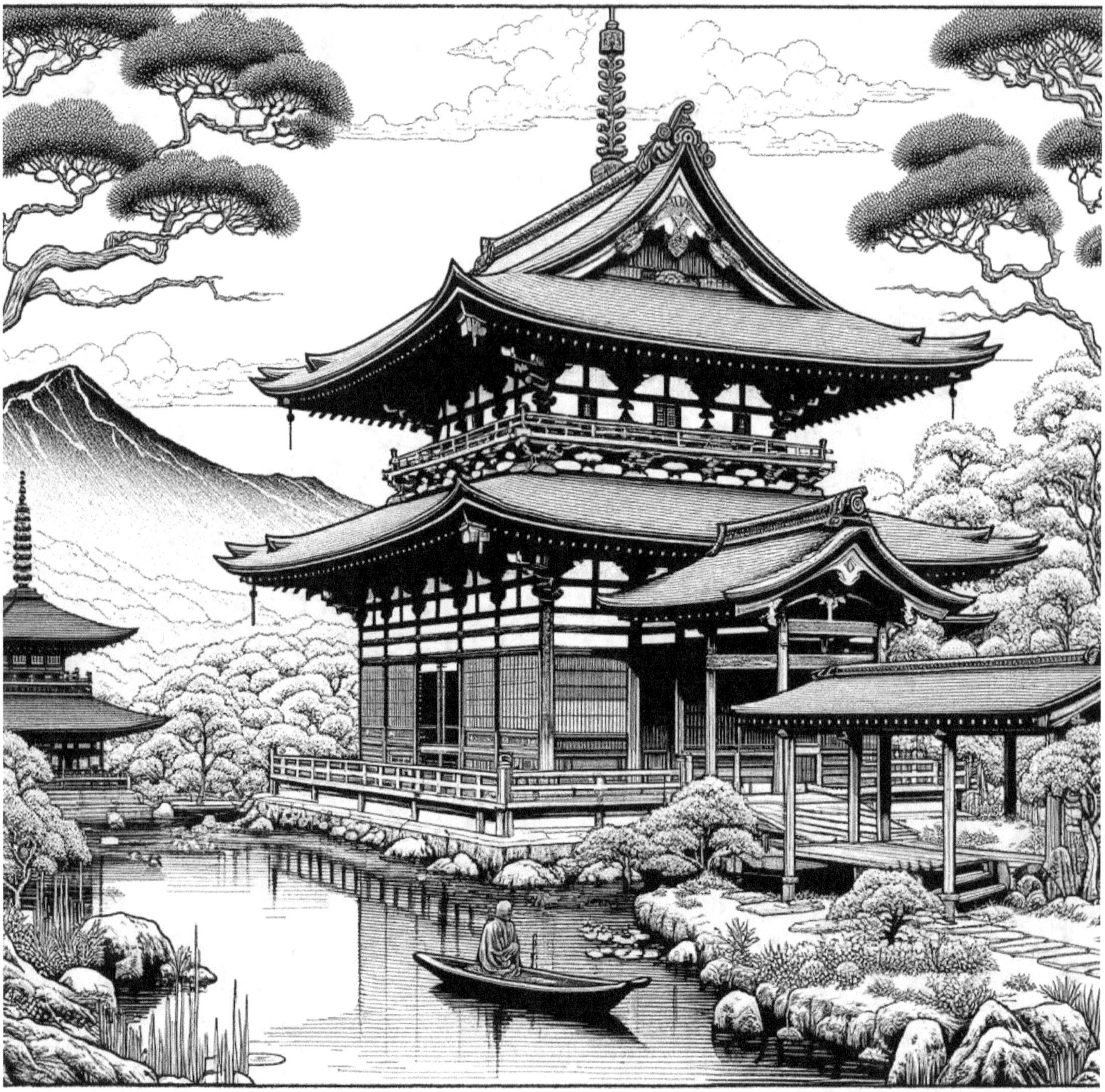

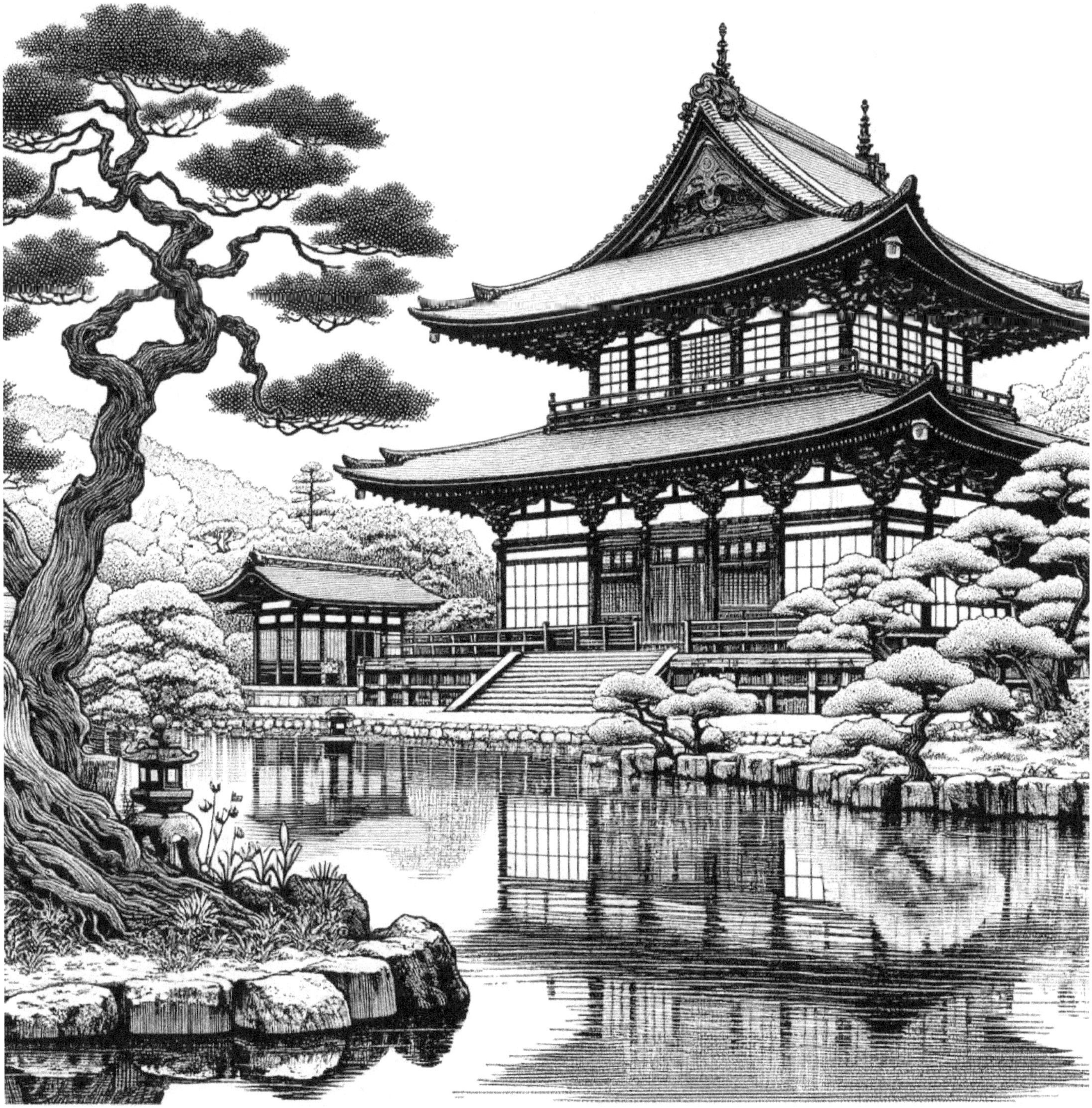

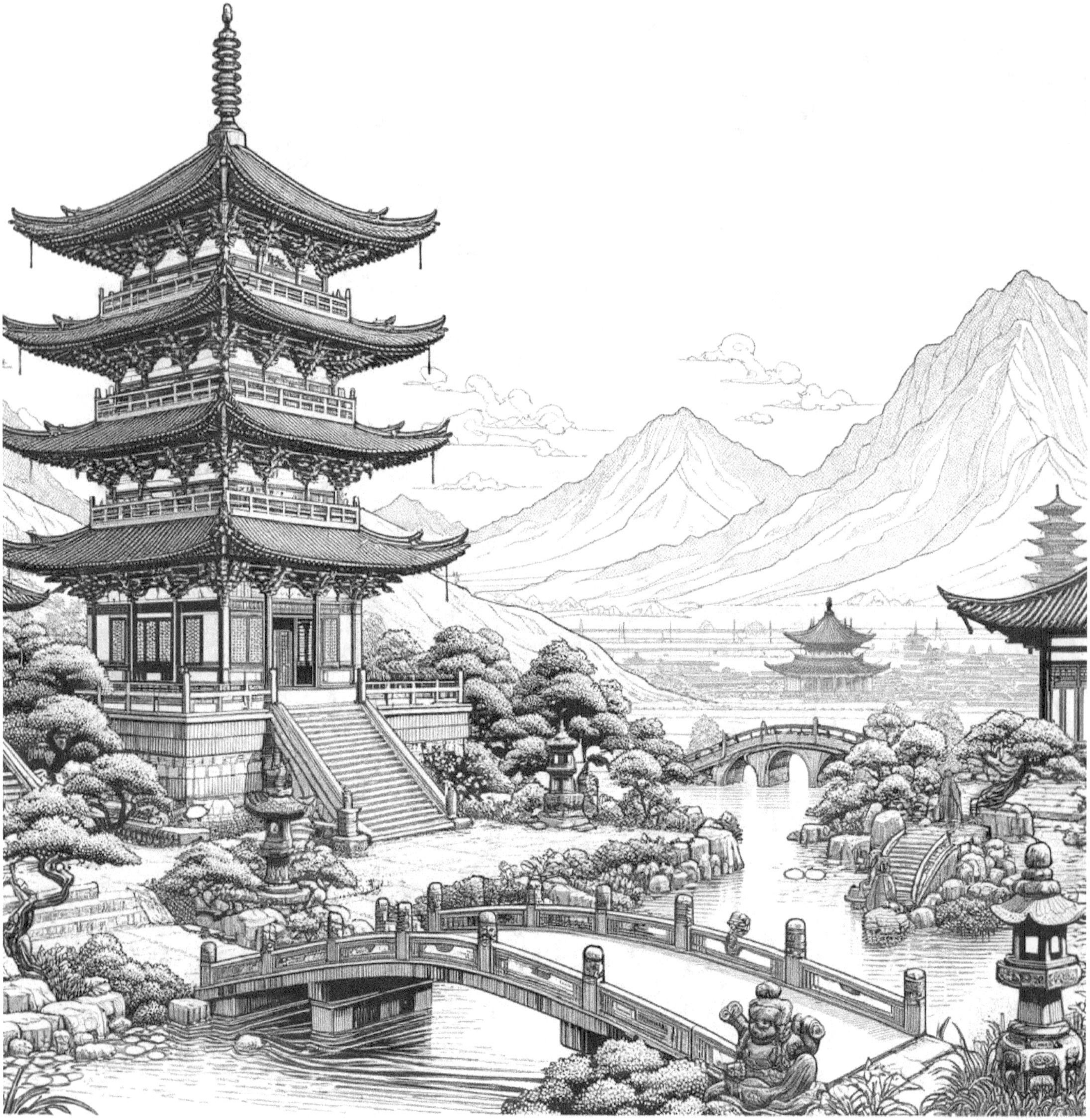

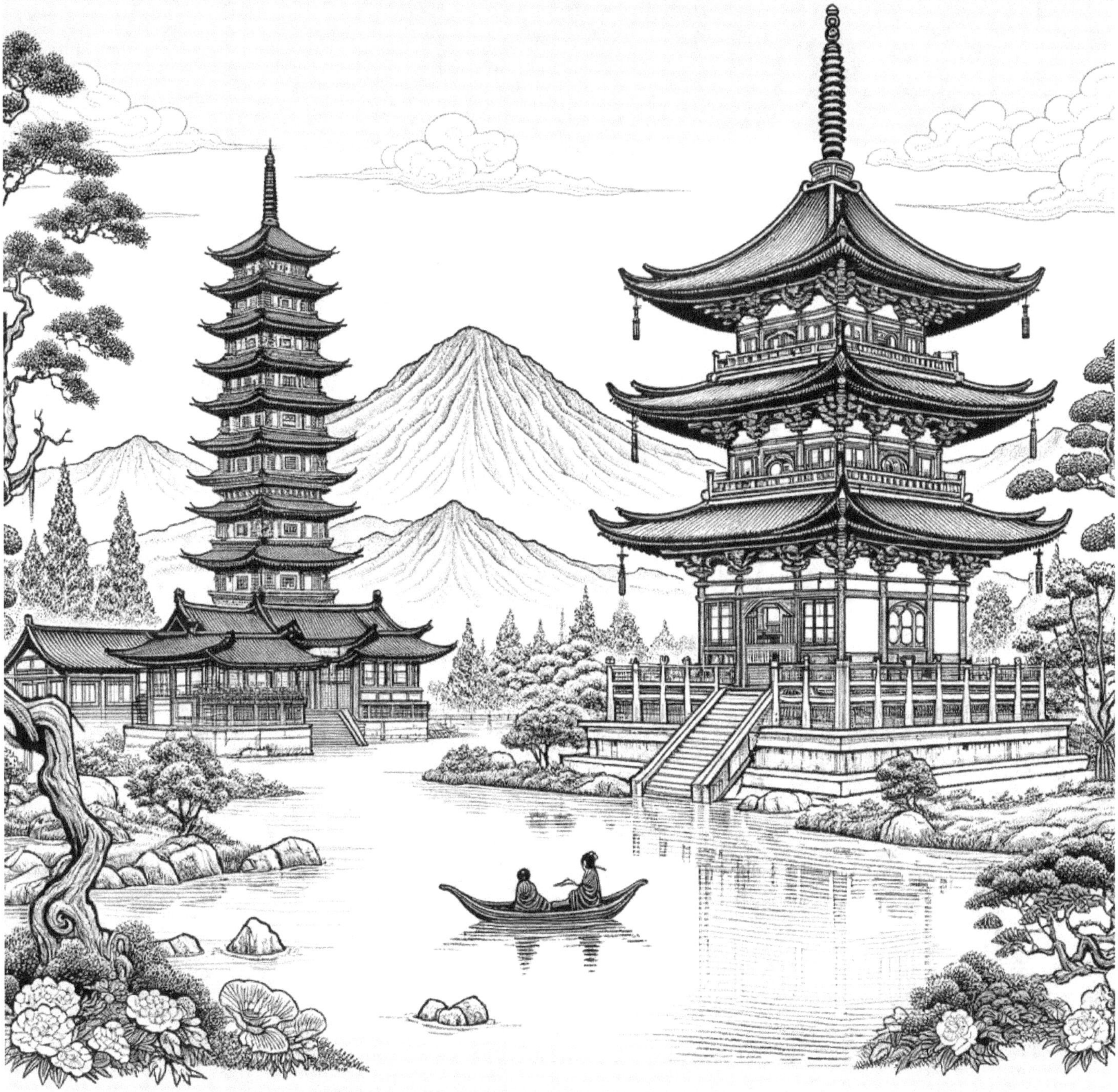

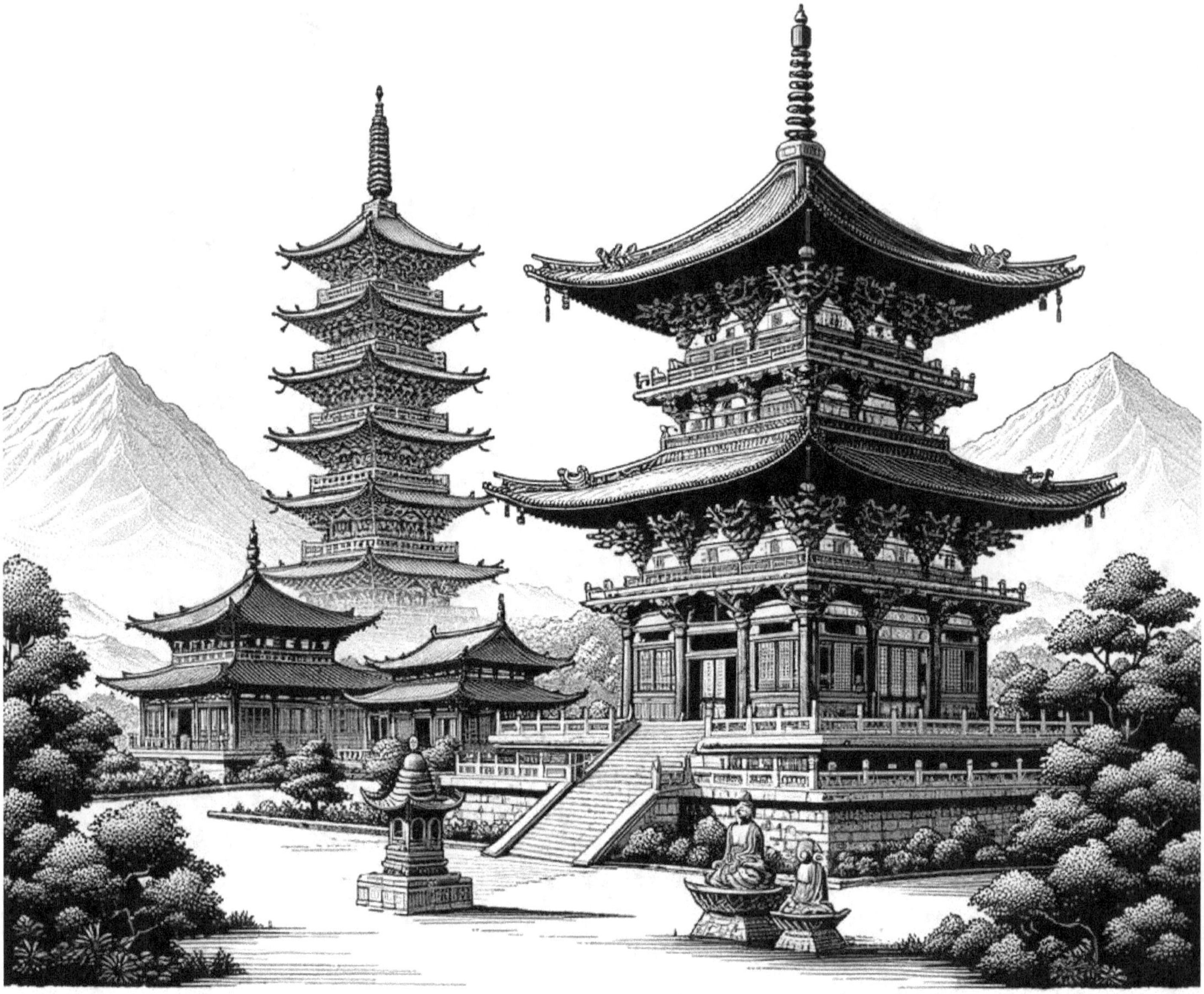

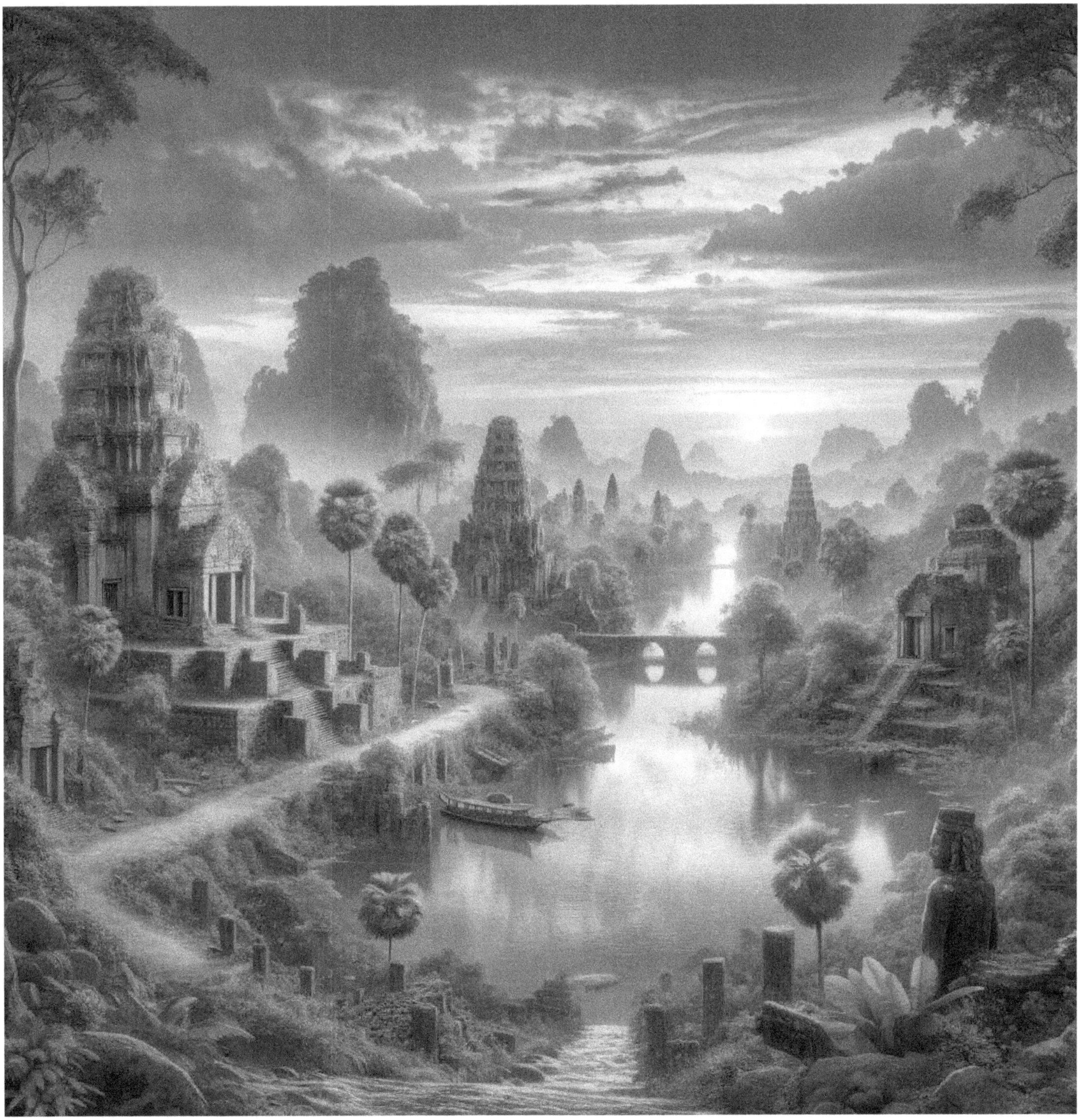

Southeast Asian Temples

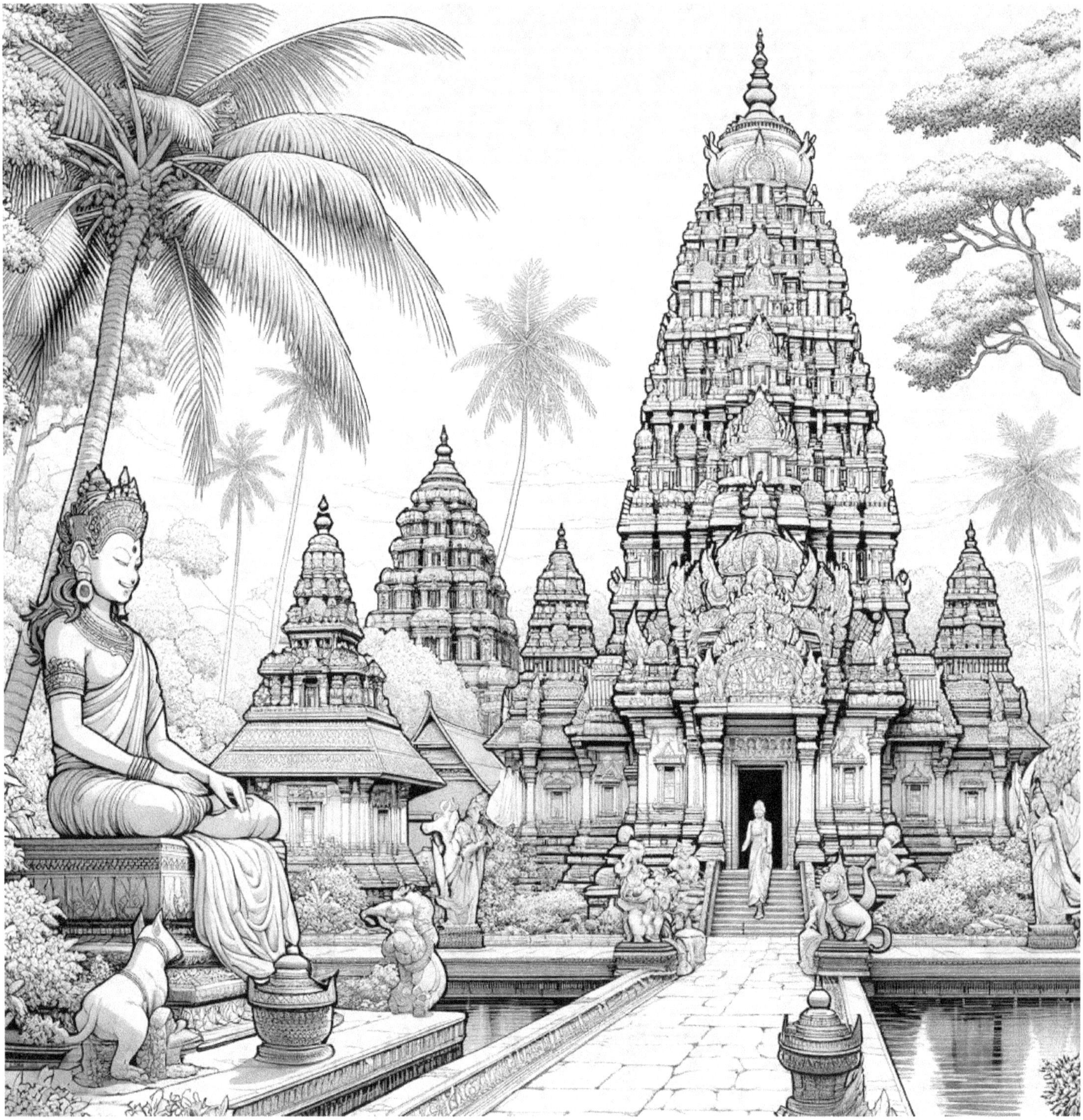

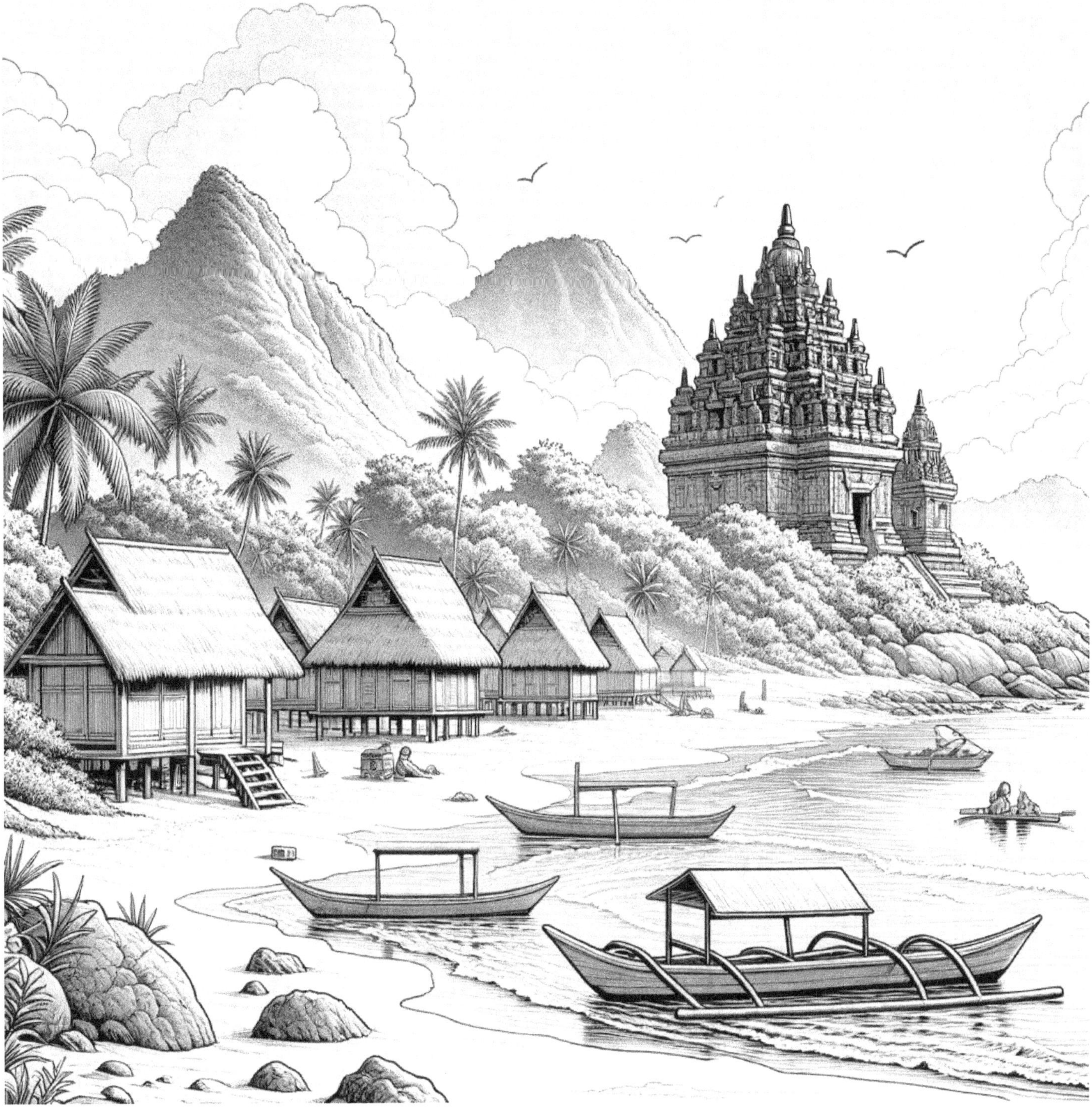

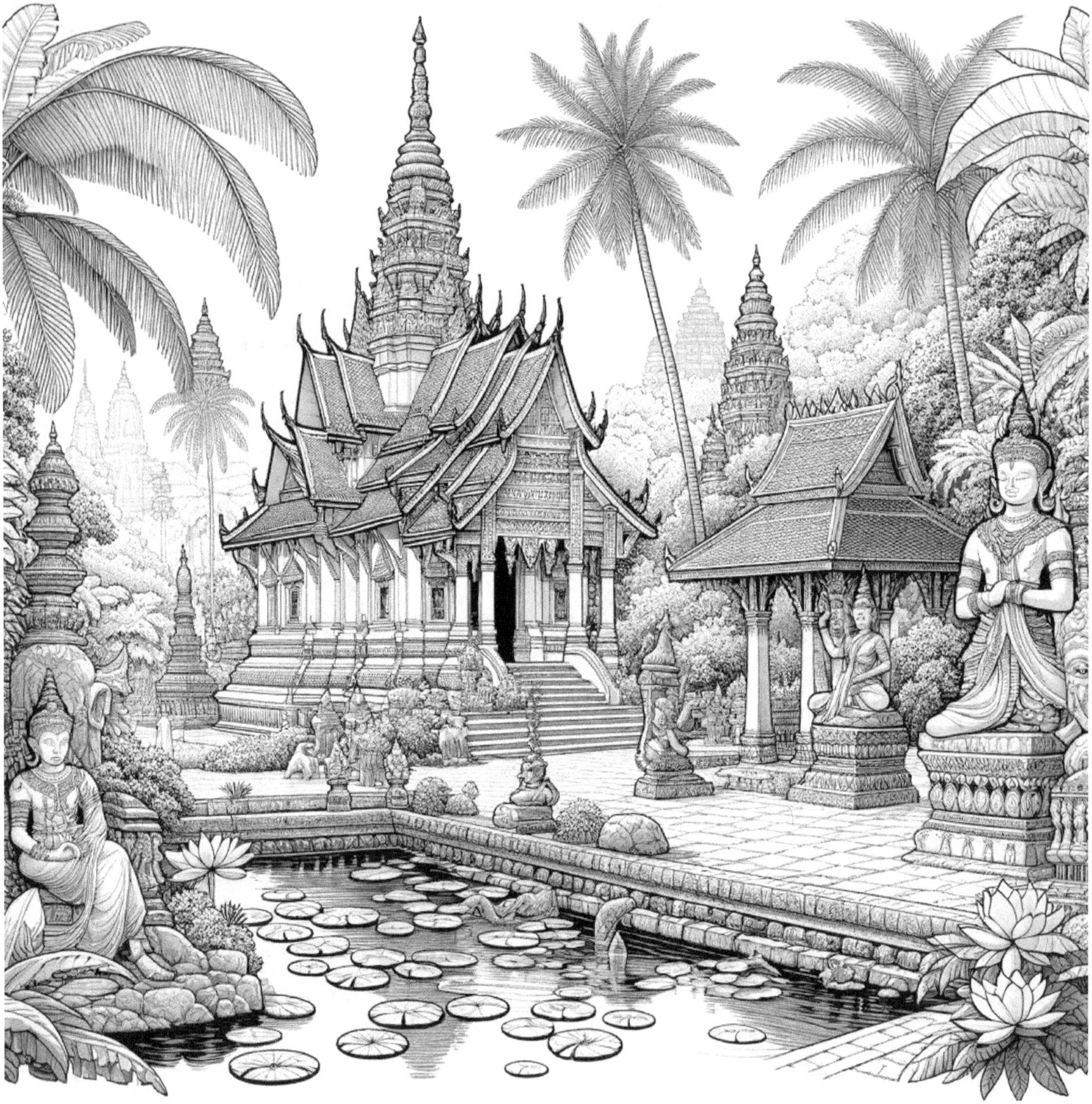

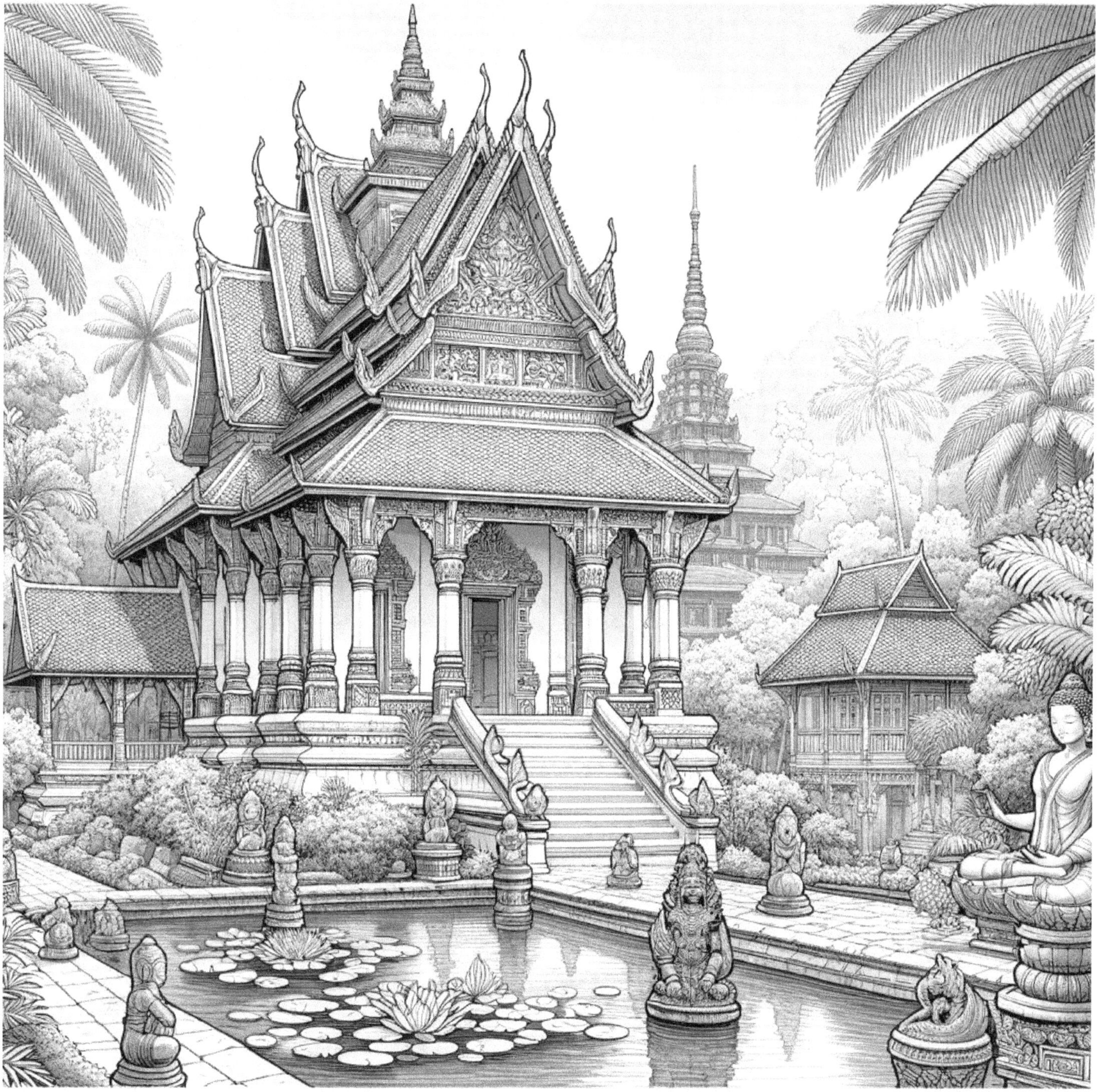

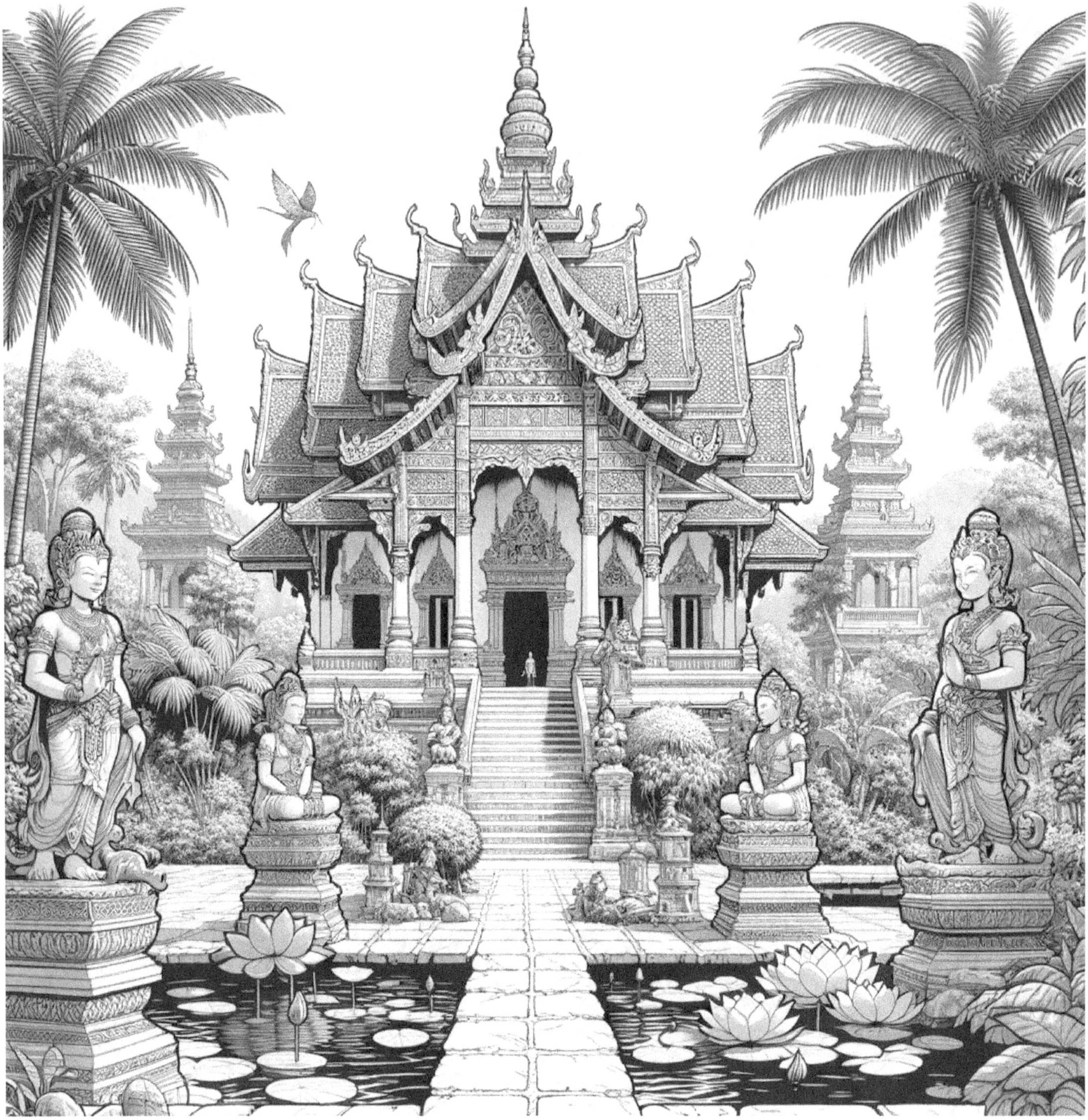

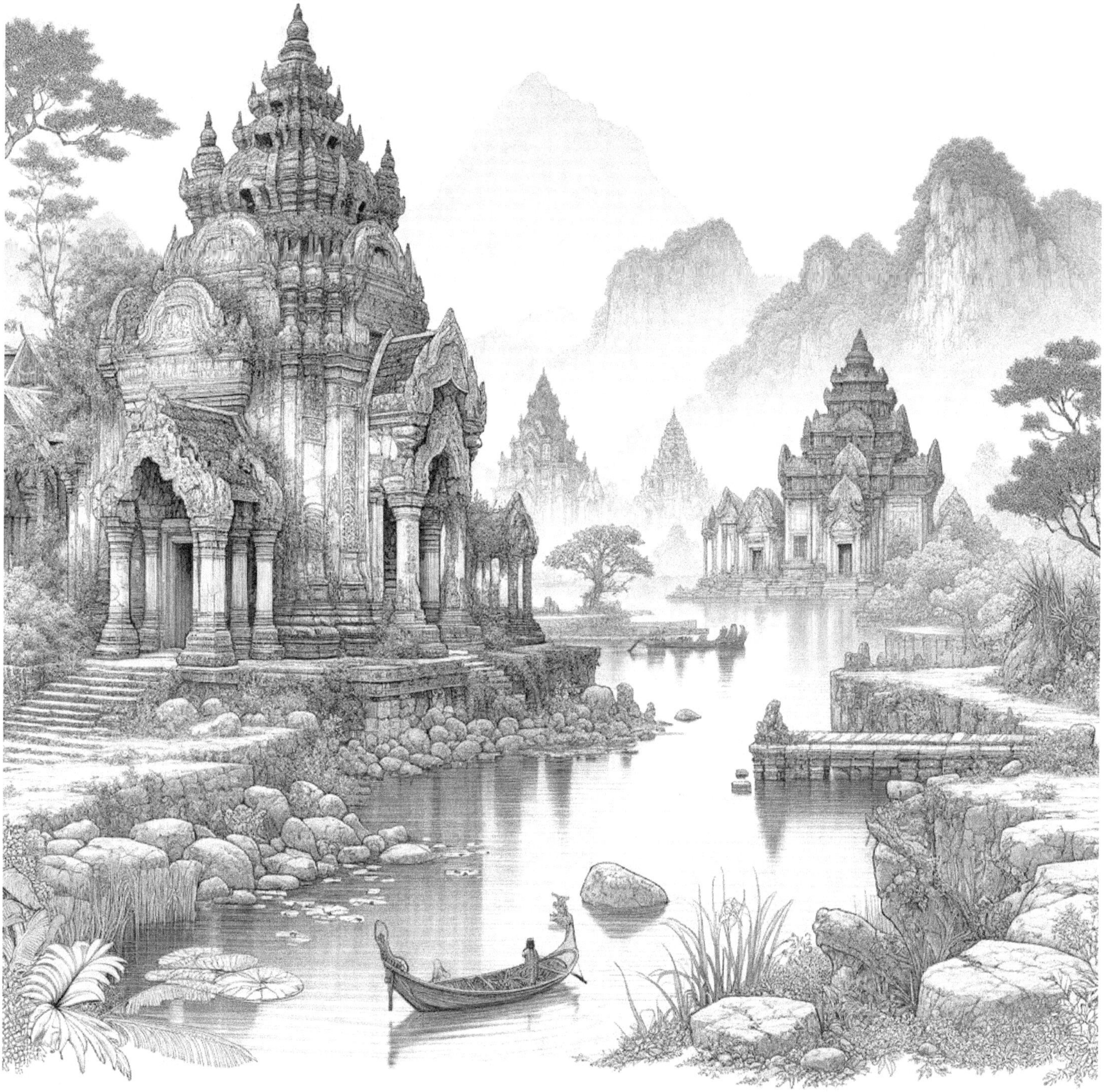

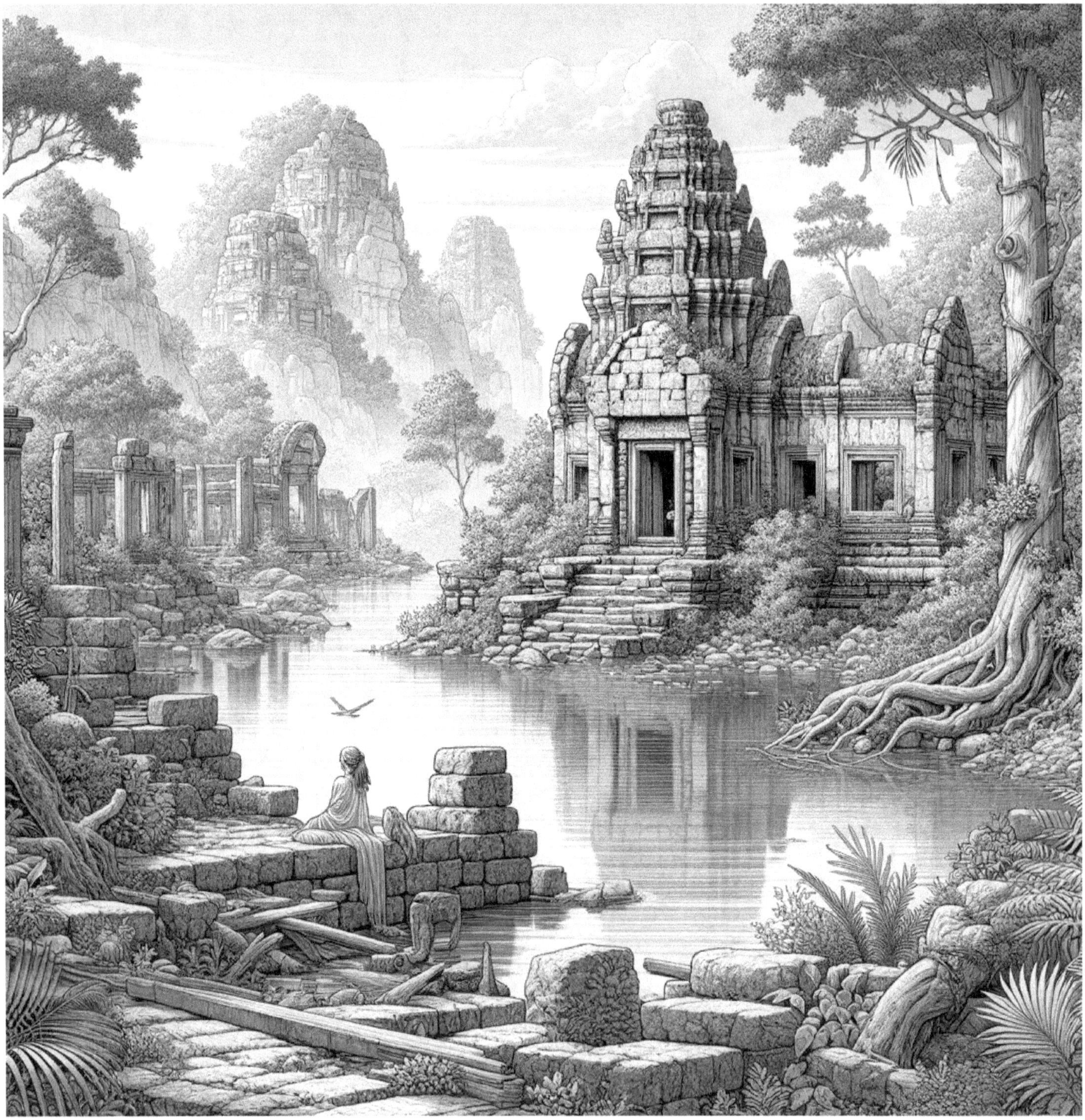

www.ingramcontent.com/pod-product-compliance
Lightning Source LLC
Chambersburg PA
CBHW080941290526
45795CB00007BA/2844
* 9 7 9 8 8 7 7 4 3 0 2 1 1 *